NANCY PELOSI

NANCY PELOSI

FIRST WOMAN SPEAKER OF THE HOUSE

Lisa Tucker McElroy

LERNER PUBLICATIONS COMPANY · MINNEAPOLIS

This book is for Zoe and Abby McElroy, two smart, wonderful girls who always remember that they can make any dream come true—even as they make the world a better place.

The images in this book are used with the permission of: AP Photo/Lawrence Jackson, p. 2; AP Photo/J. Scott Applewhite, p. 6; Courtesy of the Pelosi family, pp. 9, 10, 11, 14, 15, 17, 19, 21, 22, 30, 31; Courtesy of Timothy Russell, Trinity (Washington) University, p. 12; AP Photo/Paul Sakuma, p. 20, AP Photo/Joe Marquette, p. 24; © Chip Somodevilla/Getty Images, pp. 26, 27; © Mandel Ngan/AFP/Getty Images, p. 28; AP Photo/Chris Gardner, p. 29; AP Photo/Charles Dharapak, p. 32; © Royalty-Free/CORBIS, p. 37; © Mannie Garcia/AFP/Getty Images, p. 38.
Front cover: © Chip Somodevilla/Getty Images

Lerner Publications Company
A division of Lerner Publishing Group, Inc.
241 First Avenue North
Minneapolis, MN U.S.A. 55401

Website address: www.lernerbooks.com

Library of Congress Cataloging-in-Publication Data

McElroy, Lisa Tucker.
    Nancy Pelosi : first woman Speaker of the House / by Lisa Tucker McElroy.
        p.   cm. — (Gateway biographies)
    Includes bibliographical references and index.
    ISBN 978-0-8225-8685-2 (lib. bdg. : alk. paper)
    1.Pelosi, Nancy, 1940- —Juvenile literature. 2. Women legislators—United States—Biography—Juvenile literature. 3. Legislators—United States—Biography Juvenile literature. 4. United States. Congress. House—Speakers—Biography—Juvenile literature. I. Title.
E840.8.P37M39 2008
328.73092—dc22   2007013065

Manufactured in the United States of America
1 2 3 4 5 6 – BP – 13 12 11 10 09 08

CONTENTS

Representative Nancy Pelosi celebrates with Democratic Party well-wishers on election night, November 7, 2006. The Democrats had just won enough votes to take control of the House of Representatives, putting Pelosi in line to be the first female Speaker of the House.

The night of November 7, 2006, was a historic one for the United States. And it was a long one for Nancy Pelosi. For the first time in many years, her political party, the Democrats, had won enough elections to take control of the House of Representatives. But it was also a night to remember for another reason. Because the Democrats were going to take charge, it looked likely that the United States would soon have its first woman Speaker of the House of Representatives–Democratic congresswoman Nancy Pelosi.

Still, other things were on Pelosi's mind. Soon after she fell asleep in the wee hours of the morning, the phone rang. An aide woke her up. "Is my new grandchild here?" she asked. No, the aide replied, but the president of the United States was calling to offer his congratulations on the election. Only for Nancy Pelosi would a historic political victory, the birth of a grandchild, and a call from the president all hold equal importance.

Childhood in Baltimore

Our lives were about campaigns.
    —Nancy Pelosi

Looking back, it seemed like destiny that Nancy Patricia D'Alesandro Pelosi would become a political leader. She was born on March 26, 1940, in Baltimore, Maryland. She was the first girl after six boys, so needless to say, her parents celebrated her arrival. One of her brothers died at a young age from pneumonia. She and her five surviving brothers, Thomas (Tommy), Nicholas, Franklin Roosevelt, Hector, and Joseph (Joey), lived a very exciting childhood.

It was exciting because her father, Thomas D'Alesandro, was a politician. Nancy's childhood was all about politics. She recalls, "You [walked] into our home and were . . . given a placard or a bumper sticker or a brochure to distribute." The only days off? Christmas and Easter. Because her father was mayor of Baltimore and then a U.S. congressman for five terms, people often came to the D'Alesandro house to ask her father for help. He kept a "favor file" on a table in the front room. Nancy's job was to record in it the favors he did for people. She says that it helped her practice her penmanship.

The D'Alesandro family was Italian American. They lived in a row house (a house attached to others) in Little Italy, a part of Baltimore where many other Italian

Nancy swore in her father, Thomas D'Alesandro (left), as mayor of Baltimore in 1948.

American families had settled. She enjoyed being part of this community and knowing that her father helped people there.

Perhaps because Nancy was the only girl in the family, her father and brothers were very protective of her. She remembers that they would often interview her dates or try to convince her to stay home. "I wanted to be independent. And they were always, you know, 'Oh, you can't do this, you can't do that.' Telling me all the things I couldn't do," Pelosi said. And rebelling was not an option, she also said, because in the 1950s, children

Nancy and her mother, Annunciata D'Alesandro, work on homework together in 1950.

were expected to obey their parents without question. Smiling, she does admit that she occasionally snuck out without permission.

Nancy's father taught her a lot about politics, her eventual career. Her friend Art Torres remembers, "She has always said to me that she learned something important from her father. No matter how much you disagree with someone, always keep the friendship in your voice." Nancy took that lesson to heart. She committed herself to helping people in a courteous, kind way.

As Nancy got older, she became involved in public service in many ways. While still a teenager, she often answered the phone at home and tried to help the callers, her father's constituents, with their problems. She helped people "get . . . on welfare, into a hospital bed, into a project . . . even out of jail." It was a lot of responsibility for a teen, but Nancy enjoyed the task of helping people.

Nancy's family was Roman Catholic. She went to Mass regularly as a child. She went to a Catholic high school, the Institute of Notre Dame. She lived on campus at a Catholic college, the all-female Trinity College, in nearby Washington, D.C. It was a very big step for Nancy to live at college, as her father did

A young Nancy talks with then senator John F. Kennedy in the 1950s.

not want her to leave home. But her mother, Annunciata, stuck up for her. Annunciata had wanted to go to law school and had even taken some law classes. Because she had six children to raise, she had had to withdraw from college. Annunciata wanted her daughter to do everything she hadn't been able to do herself. Finally, Nancy's father gave in, and off she went to the nation's capital.

Nancy was an excellent student. She loved reading and books. She also enjoyed the college atmosphere. She said, "I loved Trinity College. It was an absolute joy to go there. We were in Washington, D.C., so I was active with the college Democrats. All of us . . . felt very nurtured at Trinity. Our friendships are stronger today than they were then. My best friends from Trinity are still my best friends."

Nancy attended Trinity College in Washington, D.C. The college later was known as Trinity Washington University.

The Impact of a Book

One book Nancy Pelosi read as a girl was *Cry, the Beloved Country* by South African writer Alan Paton. The book was about racism in South Africa, where black and white people lived apart in a system called apartheid. In college she took a summer school class at Georgetown University called the History of Africa South of the Sahara. Her professor was the legendary Dr. Carroll Quigley, who would also eventually teach future president Bill Clinton.

When Nancy Pelosi was given an honorary degree from Georgetown in 2002, she told the graduates: "Dr. Quigley taught us something I will never forget. He said that America is the greatest country in the history of the world because our people have always believed in two things: that tomorrow can be better than today, and that every one of us has a personal, moral responsibility to make it so."

As a congresswoman, Nancy Pelosi has been very involved in issues that affect Africa, including human rights, AIDS, poverty, trade, and debt relief. She has also led congressional trips to many places in Africa, including South Africa (land of *Cry, the Beloved Country*) and most recently Darfur, Sudan, where her group pledged to bring humanitarian aid and to help stop the killing of African people, who are being murdered for racial and political reasons.

It just goes to show how important a book can be.

> *Quite a difference one book can make in your life!*
>
> —NANCY PEL[OSI]

14

Nancy D'Alesandro married
Paul Pelosi in 1963.

Nancy's time at Trinity was exciting for another reason. It was during her years there that she met Paul Pelosi in a summer school class at Georgetown University, where he was a student. The two quickly fell in love and decided to marry. Nancy D'Alesandro became Nancy Pelosi on September 7, 1963. They had a large wedding in a Catholic church with many friends and family in attendance.

Starting a Family

My children trained me to be disciplined and to have a routine which is very helpful to this day.
   —Nancy Pelosi

Marriage was a big step. But even bigger ones were on the horizon for Nancy and Paul Pelosi. First, the couple moved to New York City for his career as a real estate investor. She then carried on a family tradition: having many children! She was pregnant for most of the 1960s. In a little more than six years of marriage, Nancy Pelosi gave birth to five beautiful children: Nancy Corinne, Christine, Jacqueline, Paul Jr., and Alexandra.

Alexandra was their only child not born in New York City. She was born in San Francisco, where the Pelosi family moved in 1969 for Paul's business. They would live in this beautiful city in California for the next several decades.

For seventeen years, Nancy concentrated on raising her five children. It was challenging but fun to be the mother of five. "Having five children puts you in a routine," she said. "It's hard to get help with five little ones at home. No one wants to take on all that. It is hard to find someone willing to come in and even watch them for a little while, so you have to take care of them yourself. And to do it, you find you have to be so efficient. You have to be organized, to

The Pelosis moved to San Francisco, California, in 1969.

keep them on schedule and get everything else done— the grocery shopping, the cooking, the laundry—it all has to be organized."

She succeeded at keeping the household organized. The family had dinner together most nights after Paul Pelosi arrived home from his office. Nancy Pelosi believed in eating healthy, balanced meals. They always had meat, a starch such as potatoes or rice, and a vegetable—she even made the children eat liver. After dinner the children would help get ready for the next meal. The children were responsible for clearing the plates, setting out cereal bowls for the next morning, and setting the table.

The Pelosi children attended Catholic schools. Their mother made sure they did their homework. On school nights, she checked to see that all the children's homework was done and their school uniforms were pressed. Often she asked the children to read their homework aloud to her while she cooked dinner. Her children remember that their mother always knew all the answers! She often told the children, "Proper preparation prevents poor performance."

To keep the household efficient, the Pelosi children even had easy-to-care-for pets: goldfish and hamsters. They had fun in lots of other ways too. Alexandra, the youngest child, remembers piling into the "way way back" of her mom's red Jeep to go to the ice-cream parlor on summer nights. "We all had brown hair and looked just alike," says Alexandra. Indeed, Nancy usually dressed

Nancy and Paul Pelosi's children in 1972. From left, they are Nancy Corinne, Christine, Jacqueline, Paul Jr., and Alexandra.

all five children in similar outfits so that she could easily spot them in a crowd.

The Pelosi family also loved to go on vacation. Every summer the entire family went to Ocean City, Maryland, to visit the D'Alesandro family. The children would play games on the boardwalk with their uncles and their cousins, play on the beach, and enjoy family dinners at Phillips Crab House almost every night. Most winters they went skiing in Lake Tahoe, California. They would all drive together in the family car for the three-and-one-half-hour trip.

Nancy Pelosi devoted most of her time to raising her children. Still, she never lost the political "bug." She often volunteered to raise campaign funds for Democrats running for office. She eventually was appointed a member of the Democratic National Committee, a political organization that supports candidates for office and tries to raise awareness on important issues. Her children remember that she was always home when they got home from school. They would know that she had been out during the day, though, because she would bring home chocolate desserts from Just Desserts, her favorite bakery. They also remember that if one of them was sick and needed to be picked up, the school knew that San Francisco's headquarters for the Democratic Party was the place to call to find Nancy Pelosi. On their days off from school, they visited the headquarters with their mom. The children wanted to have fun with the office supplies. But their mother wanted them to help Democratic candidates by stuffing envelopes. They usually struck a deal. If the kids helped with the campaigns, their mother would give them money to go across the street to Liberty House to buy the best french onion soup in town. The children usually agreed to help.

As her children grew, Nancy Pelosi became more and more involved with the Democratic Party. For example, in 1984, she was in charge of the Host Committee for the Democratic National Convention in San Francisco. Soon after, she became the chairperson of the California Democratic Party.

Still, it was not until 1987—when her youngest child was a high school senior—that Nancy Pelosi decided to run for political office. When she did, she did it big. She ran for a seat in the U.S. House of Representatives, representing the Fifth Congressional District of California. The district, later renamed the Eighth District, includes most of the city of San Francisco.

Paul Pelosi was surprised at, but supportive of, her decision to run for office. "It wasn't even on the table. It wasn't even part of the discussion. Nothing in her personality—it was never going to happen," he has said. But the two agreed that if she won, they would have a bicoastal marriage. Nancy Pelosi would spend weekdays in Washington, D.C., and then return on weekends. Her husband would visit Washington every month or so. And

The Pelosi family in 1987: (left to right) Nancy Corinne, Alexandra, Paul Jr., Nancy, Jacqueline, Paul, and Christine

Nancy Pelosi waves to her supporters at her campaign headquarters in San Francisco on April 7, 1987, the night of her election to the U.S. House of Representatives.

they would keep in close touch with constant phone calls. Nancy Pelosi won the election. A new phase of her life began as she headed off to the nation's capital.

Early Days in Congress

I didn't come here to hang out.
    —Nancy Pelosi

When Nancy Pelosi went to work in Washington, she was in it to work hard. She was forty-seven years old.

She had spent most of her adult life raising children. In Congress she wanted to make a difference for children across the United States. "I thought my work in politics was a continuation of caring for my family," she said. "It is all about the children. It is about working on things and having an impact on families. There are things you can do as a parent but then you reach a point where there are things you can't do unless you are in public service. You can't ensure the quality of the air they breathe is healthy, or the water they drink is clear of harmful chemicals, or guarantee them a world at peace or relate to other nations and ensure their well being unless you are in public service. So I believe that my public service is a continuation of my life as a mom."

From her early days as a congresswoman, Pelosi got to know colleagues from all over the country. She made friends and allies by learning about their stories. She knew all about their families, where they went to

Nancy Pelosi (left) and her father (seated) at her House of Representatives swearing in ceremony on June 9, 1987.

school, what hobbies they had outside of work, and what sports teams they liked. She became known as a good listener and someone who never forgot a favor. And she worked hard on the issues she cared about: peace, education, health care, the environment, and equal rights for all.

During these early years, Pelosi flew back and forth to San Francisco every weekend. She flew in the coach section, often sitting in a window seat, rarely being recognized. But it was important to her to go home to her husband, Paul, and to visit the people who elected her in California.

As the years went by, Pelosi became more and more respected in her party. Pelosi's hard work and commitment were apparent to her colleagues. In 2001 they elected her the party whip, or second in command among House Democrats. She was the first woman ever to hold such a high post in Congress.

The Pelosi family together in the late 1980s. From left, back row: Paul, Alexandra, Christine, Nancy; from left, front row: Nancy Corinne, Paul Jr., Jacqueline.

Mother-of-Five Voice

When Nancy Pelosi speaks to large crowds, they often clap and cheer. Pelosi tries to quiet them so that she can speak. Sometimes, though, they just won't quiet down. When that happens, she's apt to say, "Do I need to use my mother-of-five voice?"

Pelosi and her friends believe that her experience as a mom has really helped her in her political career. She knows how to be polite but firm. She knows how to multitask and get things done. She knows that honesty and civility are essential. And she knows that chocolate can get pretty much anyone through the day.

In response to being told that her management style is motherly, she has said, "I guess it depends on your definition of motherly. If motherly means—we'll have order in the house, yes." Being in politics isn't a tea party, says Pelosi (and she should know, given that she has had quite a few with her daughters and granddaughters). Sometimes you have to get tough. You have to have a thick skin. And who's tougher than your average mom?

> *To me, the center of my life will always be raising my family. It is the complete joy of my life. To me, working in Congress is a continuation of that.*
>
> —NANCY PELOSI

Nancy Pelosi adds a touch of humor by posing with an actual whip to celebrate her election as the party whip for the House Democrats in 2001.

In her first year as whip, she visited thirty states to campaign and fund-raise for Democrats. She encouraged people to vote and to base their votes on issues that they cared about, such as education, the war, and the environment. Despite her important job, few people recognized her. Her male colleagues sometimes referred to her as "a little girl from California." Pelosi ignored the lack of recognition. As she had told her children for many years, she thought she could get more done if she didn't mind giving up the credit for doing the job.

At the end of 2002, after the House minority leader— the leader of the party not in power in the House— stepped down to run for president, Pelosi's colleagues were solidly behind her filling that vacancy. She got 177 of 206 votes to make her minority leader of the House. In the four years she held that post, the United States faced many crises: the war on terrorism, Hurricane Katrina, and problems with the economy and education. Pelosi worked long days during these years, sponsoring bills (suggesting and supporting new laws), fund-raising, and making speeches. Her style? A colleague has called her leadership style "the chocolate and the gavel." During her career, she delivered chocolate cakes to allies and staffers, and she kept a bowl of Ghirardelli choco- lates (from San Francisco, of course) on her desk. And as her party's leader in the House, she banged her gavel many times. Her goal? To work toward the Democrats once again having a majority in the House and to solve what she saw as the nation's problems.

And then it happened. All her hard work paid off, and the goal she had been working toward for so many years was realized. On November 7, 2006, the Democrats regained the majority in the House. On November 16, 2006, the Democratic members of the House unani- mously elected her to be their candidate for Speaker, the leader of the House of Representatives.

Nancy Pelosi's fellow Democrats chose her as their candidate for Speaker of the House on November 16, 2006.

The Swearing In

From the kitchen to the Congress!
   —Nancy Pelosi

On January 4, 2007, the election for Speaker took place. The Speaker is elected by *viva voce*, or "voice vote." This means that each member of Congress announces a choice for Speaker out loud. A clerk records the result. To be elected, the Speaker must receive a majority of the votes of the members present. She beat out the

Republican candidate, John Boehner, by a vote of 233–202. The United States had its first woman Speaker. Her colleagues' cheers were incredibly loud. They almost drowned out the clerk's announcement of the House's voice vote!

The former Speaker symbolically handed Pelosi the Speaker's gavel. The entire House, even the Republicans, stood up to applaud her. They knew that the election of

Nancy Pelosi shows off the Speaker's gavel (hammerlike instrument) after being elected the first female Speaker of the House on January 4, 2007.

the first woman Speaker was a historic moment!

Pelosi's children and grandchildren were all present. Her newest grandchild, baby Paul, slept through the whole ceremony. The other grandchildren all came up to the podium to join their grandmother and touch the gavel. Soon, children and grandchildren of other House members came up to join them.

Nancy Pelosi is surrounded by her grandchildren as well as children and grandchildren of other House members during her swearing in as Speaker of the House on January 4, 2007.

Nancy Pelosi (center) and her husband, Paul, (left) laugh as her brother, Thomas D'Alesandro III (right) speaks January 5, 2007, during one of the events in Baltimore celebrating Nancy Pelosi's election as Speaker of the House.

Pelosi celebrated for three days after the election. She honored her Italian heritage with a party at the Italian Embassy. She visited her college, Trinity College. She held an open house that included a tour of Congress. The famous singer Tony Bennett serenaded her with "I Left My Heart in San Francisco." Perhaps most significantly for Pelosi, she attended Mass to thank God and ask for guidance in her new role.

Being a Grandmother

While Nancy Pelosi has been serving in Congress, other exciting things have been happening in her life. In 1997 she became a grandmother with the birth of her first grandchild, Alexander. Since then she has welcomed five more grandchildren: Madeline, Liam, Ryan, Sean, and Paul. All the grandchildren call Pelosi "Mimi." They see her every few months, especially on special occasions. She visits whenever she can, and they visit her in San Francisco and Washington, D.C. Together, they do the things that most grandparents and grandchildren do. They play games, swim, do puzzles, go on nature walks, and . . . eat chocolate! "Mimi" Pelosi loves to attend her grandchildren's games— she's the loudest fan there! At one recent football game where her grandson Alexander was a player, she was one

Nancy and Paul Pelosi have six grandchildren, five of whom are shown in this 2003 photo. Back row, left to right: Alexander, Nancy Pelosi ("Mimi"), Madeleine; front row, left to right: Liam, Sean, Paul Pelosi ("Pop"), Ryan.

Nancy and Paul Pelosi welcomed their sixth grand-child Paul Michael on November 13, 2006.

of the fans who stayed out longest to cheer in the rain.

Pelosi likes to have all her grandchildren together twice a year, at Thanksgiving and during the summer. And when she's not with them? There's always the telephone.

It's great. It's fabulous. It was my goal in life and now I've achieved it. I'm a grandmother.

—NANCY PELOS[

THE SPEAKER OF THE HOUSE

The U.S. Constitution, the document on which the laws of the United States are based, established the role of Speaker, but it did not dictate the Speaker's duties. Those responsibilities have evolved over the course of U.S. history.

> *They say 'Madam' ...but you can call me Nancy.*
>
> —NANCY PELO

As Speaker, Nancy Pelosi presides over the House of Representatives and administers House rules. She appoints and selects members for committees. She often leads negotiations with the Senate and the president. She also helps solve conflicts within her own political party.

As Speaker, Nancy Pelosi is also a regular member of Congress. She still represents the Eighth District of California. However, as Speaker, she rarely votes or speaks on the floor of the House of Representatives.

A male Speaker is addressed as "Mr. Speaker." Our first woman Speaker? Officially, she's "Madam Speaker"—but she prefers just plain "Nancy."

Nancy Pelosi has many duties as Speaker of the House, including hitting the table with a gavel to call the sessions to order.

The Speaker's Job

Let us join together in the first 100 hours to make this Congress the most honest and open Congress in history.
    —Nancy Pelosi

After all the celebrating was over, it was time to get to work. Pelosi had several major tasks to accomplish. She told Congress that its first one hundred hours of business under her leadership were going to be productive and important. She wanted to raise the minimum wage (or the smallest amount of money that every American worker must earn) and increase certain kinds of scientific research. She wanted to make the country safer after the 9/11 attacks. She wanted to make college more affordable for young adults. She wanted to make prescription drugs more affordable for elderly patients. And she wanted to make sure that Congress would spend only the money it had in the bank.

Pelosi's list was long and challenging. Many people thought she could not accomplish it in one hundred weeks or one hundred years—much less one hundred hours. But it took only forty-two hours for Pelosi to bring Congress together to pass laws to make significant progress on all these goals.

The first hundred hours were only a warm-up for Pelosi. The hard work lies ahead. For example, on a typical day when the House is in session, Pelosi is up very early—often as early as four thirty or five in the morning.

After she looks over papers from her office and makes some phone calls, she usually has an early breakfast meeting with staffers or other members of Congress. Sometimes she even eats chocolate ice cream for breakfast! Then she opens the House of Representatives at ten o'clock.

To "open the House," Pelosi walks into the chambers of the House of Representatives. The sergeant at arms carries the four-foot-long (122-centimeter) silver and ebony mace of the House in front of the Speaker in procession. This ornamental staff is one of the oldest symbols of the U.S. government. They walk to the rostrum—the area with the Speaker's chair and the Speaker's gavel. Pelosi goes to the Speaker's chair, takes the gavel, bangs it on the rostrum, and calls the House to order. The chaplain leads a prayer, and then Pelosi calls upon a member of Congress to lead the Pledge of Allegiance. After this ceremony, the workday begins with debates on legislation or speeches by members of Congress.

From there, her day gets even busier. She holds meetings in her office, which is decorated with flowering plants. She has lots and lots of meetings: with organizations, staffers, other members of the House, and visiting foreign officials. She often presides over votes in the House chamber. She gives speeches for many organizations and attends many parties and receptions. She usually manages to squeeze in a toasted tuna sandwich on wheat bread for lunch and makes time for calls to her husband back in San Francisco, children, and grandchildren. And, of course, she snacks on chocolate all day, every day.

TWO HEARTBEATS AWAY

Ask most people what would happen if the president died or could not serve out the term? They'd tell you that the vice president would take over, and they'd be right. But what if the vice president couldn't serve, either? Well, then our next president would be a woman: Nancy Pelosi. That's because the Speaker of the House is second in the line of succession to the presidency of the United States. Some people call this position being "two heartbeats away," because the death of the president and vice president (while an unlikely event) would result in the Speaker taking the oath of office as president. When the American people voted on November 7, 2006, many of them did so knowing that Nancy Pelosi would become Speaker and that they were possibly setting the stage for the first woman president of the United States.

If, by reason of death, resignation, removal from office, inability, or failure to qualify, there is neither a President nor Vice President to discharge the powers and duties of the office of President, then the Speaker of the House of Representatives shall, upon his resignation as Speaker and as Representative in Congress, act as President.

—PRESIDENTIAL SUCCESSION ACT OF 1947

Breaking the Marble Ceiling

For many years, American women have been taking on important jobs outside the home. Whenever a woman achieves something new or exciting in the workplace, it is called "breaking the glass ceiling." When Nancy Pelosi became the first woman Speaker, though, she said she'd broken the marble ceiling, perhaps because of all the marble in the Capitol Building. "You have to understand. . . . This makes glass look like nothing. This is a marble ceiling," she said. "I believe [that in] that highly visible role [I can] show the American people that women know how to use power, that I think it helps all women in the political process or whatever field they're in. . . . I think it will be a plus."

It wasn't always that way. When she first visited the White House, she was the only woman in an important meeting. But then she realized she wasn't alone. She has said, "I realized I was surrounded in my chair by [early woman's rights leaders] Susan B. Anthony and Elizabeth Cady Stanton . . . and I could almost hear them say, 'We want more.' Of course, my first thought was that we [all] want more."

Because Nancy Pelosi has become the highest-ranking woman ever in the U.S. government, many girls and women look up to her. Fathers of daughters have come up to her to

> *At last, we have a seat at the table.*
>
> —NANCY PELO[SI]

The Capitol building in Washington, D.C.

say, "I want my daughter to meet you because I want her to know that anything is possible for her."

And in her acceptance speech upon becoming Speaker, Nancy Pelosi addressed the victory head-on. "This is an historic moment—for the Congress, and for the women of this country. It is a moment for which we have waited more than 200 years. Never losing faith, we waited through the many years of struggle to achieve our rights. But women weren't just waiting; women were working. Never losing faith, we worked to redeem the promise of America, that all men and women are created equal. For our daughters and granddaughters, today we have broken the marble ceiling."

Leading into the Future

Now it is our responsibility to carry forth that vision of a new America into the 21st century.
     —Nancy Pelosi

As Speaker, Pelosi is recognized more often than she used to be. She has less privacy, and many people want to talk to her. They are excited that the United States has its first woman Speaker.

Pelosi knows that she is in a position to prove that women can govern just as well as men. She wants to unify Congress. She wants political parties to work together to make the country a better place.

"I am filled with hope," says Pelosi. "I know America's best days are ahead."

Nancy Pelosi speaks to a group of U.S. mayors at a conference in January 2007.

Fun Facts about Nancy Pelosi

- Nancy Pelosi likes designer suits, but she hates shopping. Her husband, Paul, usually shops for her.
- Pelosi loves chocolate, especially Ghirardelli chocolate and New York Super Fudge Chunk ice cream. She eats it at all times of the day.
- Pelosi does not sleep much—she says she has too much to do.
- Pelosi watches MTV and the television program *Jeopardy.*
- Pelosi does not swear and does not like people who do. She believes in being polite.
- Pelosi doesn't drink coffee with caffeine. She prefers hot water with lemon.
- When Pelosi was raising her family in San Francisco, they lived across the street from Dianne Feinstein who later became one of the U.S. senators from California.
- Pelosi loves doing crossword puzzles. She does at least one a day.
- In addition to being the first woman Speaker, Pelosi is the first Italian American and the first Californian to be elected Speaker.
- Nancy Pelosi was also the first woman whip and the first woman leader of a major political party in the House.

- Nancy Pelosi loves her cell phone. She uses it constantly to call her children and grand-children. She says she doesn't know what she ever did without it!
- Nancy Pelosi has a city street named after her in Baltimore.
- Not only was Nancy Pelosi's father mayor of Baltimore, her brother was too. Thomas J. D'Alesandro III served as mayor for four years.
- As a child, Nancy Pelosi swore in her father as mayor of Baltimore.
- Nancy and Paul Pelosi are great dancers.
- Nancy Pelosi's favorite movies are *Traffic, Gladiator,* and *Shrek.* She and her husband love to go to the movies and see two in a row when they have time.
- Nancy Pelosi's very best friend is her older brother Tommy. She talks to him on the phone every day.

CHRONOLOGY

1940   Nancy Patricia D'Alesandro is born on March 26 in Baltimore, Maryland.

1962   She graduates from Trinity College in Washington, D.C.

1963   On September 7, she marries Paul Pelosi.

1984   She chairs the Democratic National Convention Host Committee.

1987   She successfully runs for a seat in the U.S. House of Representatives.

2001   On October 11, she is elected minority whip.

2002   She is elected minority leader.

2006   Democrats recapture a majority in the House of Representatives on November 7.

   On November 16, she is unanimously elected Democratic candidate for Speaker of the House of Representatives.

2007   On January 4, she is sworn in as the first woman Speaker of the House.

GLOSSARY

Congress: the lawmaking branch of the U.S. government. Congress is made up of two houses, the House of Representatives and the Senate.

constituents: the people of a voting district whom an elected official represents

in session: a period of time when members of Congress are actively meeting in Washington, D.C.

midterm election: a congressional election occurring two years after a presidential election, or in the middle of a president's term

minority leader: the head of the political party that is not in power in the House of Representatives

Speaker: the head of the House of Representatives; usually a member of the majority party

staffer: a person who works for a member of Congress

succession: the order in which one person after another takes over a job or office

whip: a political party's second in command in the House of Representatives

SOURCE NOTES

7 Bob Herbert, "Ms. Speaker and Other Trends," *New York Times,* November 9, 2006, sec. A.

8 Adam Clymer, "A New Vote Counter: Nancy Patricia Pelosi," *New York Times,* October 11, 2001, sec. A.

8 Ibid.

8 Karen Breslau, Eleanor Clift, and Daren Briscoe, "Rolling with Pelosi," *Newsweek,* October 23, 2006, available online at *MSNBC,* 2007, http://www.msnbc.msn.com/id/15268408/site/newsweek/ (March 21, 2007).

10–11 David Firestone, "Getting Closer to the Top, and Smiling All the Way," *New York Times,* November 10, 2002, sec. 1.

11 Clymer.

12 Christine Pelosi, e-mail to the author, March 20, 2007.

13 Christine Pelosi, e-mail.

14 Alexandra Pelosi, interview with the author, March 16, 2007.

14 Peggy Lewis, "Profile: Nancy Pelosi '62, House Democratic Leader," *Trinity University Magazine,* Fall 2002, n.d., http://www.trinitydc.edu/

admissions/magazine_profile_pelosi.php (May 25, 2007).

16 Ibid.

16 Christine Pelosi, interview, and Leslie Stahl profile, *60 Minutes,* report at http://www.cbsnews.com/stories/2006/10/20/60minutes/main2111089.shtml.

16 Alexandra Pelosi, interview.

19 Stahl.

20 Kate Zernike, "Nancy Pelosi Is Ready to Be the Voice of the Majority," *New York Times,* November 9, 2006, sect. A.

21 Lewis.

23 Sally Jacobs, "Woman of the House," *Boston Globe,* February 5, 2003, sect. D.

23 Stahl.

25 Marc Sandalow, "Pelosi's House Ascending," *San Francisco Chronicle,* November 3, 2002, http://www.sfgate.com/cgi-bin/article.cgi?file=/chronicle/archive/2002/11/03/MN154974.DTL (May 25, 2007).

25 Zernike.

25 Jennifer Steinhauer, "With the House in the Balance, Pelosi Serves as a Focal Point for Both Parties," *New York Times,* October 30, 2006.

26 Nancy Pelosi, speech, January 4, 2007, *San Francisco Chronicle* n.d., http://www.sfgate.com/cgi-bin/article.cgi?f=/c/a/2007/01/04/BAG5ANCTQ27.DTL. (March 20, 2007).

31 Stahl.

32 Andrea Stone, "Pelosi to Be the First Woman to Lead Congress," *USA Today,* November 9, 2006.

33 Nancy Pelosi, speech, January 4, 2007, Speaker Nancy Pelosi, n.d., http://www.speaker.gov/newsroom/speeches?id=0006 (March 21, 2007).

36 Steinhauer.

36 Stahl.

36 Sandalow.

37 Eleanor Clift, "Fast Chat," *Newsweek*, December 30, 2002, 7.

37 Nancy Pelosi, press release, January 2007, *United States House of Representatives,* n.d. http://www.house.gov/pelosi/press/releases/Jan07/FloorSpeech.html (March 20, 2007).

38 Ibid.

38 Ibid.

SELECTED BIBLIOGRAPHY

Breslau, Karen, Eleanor Clift, and Daren Briscoe. "Rolling with Pelosi." *Newsweek*, October 23, 2006. Available online at MSNBC, 2007, http://www.msnbc.msn.com/id/15268408/site/newsweek/ (March 21, 2007).

Clift, Eleanor. "Fast Chat." *Newsweek*, December 30, 2002, 7.

Clymer, Adam. "A New Vote Counter: Nancy Patricia Pelosi." *New York Times*, October 11, 2001, sect. A.

Firestone, David. "Getting Closer to the Top, and Smiling All the Way." *New York Times*, November 10, 2002, sect. 1.

Herbert, Bob. "Ms. Speaker and Other Trends." *New York Times*, November 9, 2006, sect. A.

Jacobs, Sally. "Woman of the House." *Boston Globe*, February 5, 2003, sect. D.

Lewis, Peggy. "Profile: Nancy Pelosi '62, House Democratic Leader." *Trinity University Magazine*, Fall 2002. Available online at *Trinity Washington University*. n.d. http://www.trinitydc.edu/admissions/magazine_profile_pelosi.php (May 25, 2007).

Steinhauer, Jennifer. "With the House in the Balance, Pelosi Serves as a Focal Point for Both Parties." *New York Times*, October 30, 2006.

Stone, Andrea. "Pelosi to Be the First Woman to Lead Congress." *USA Today,* November 9, 2006.

Zernike, Kate. "Nancy Pelosi Is Ready to Be the Voice of the Majority," *New York Times*, November 9, 2006, sect. A.

FURTHER READING

There are no other books for young readers about Nancy Pelosi.

Feldman, Ruth Tenzer. *How Congress Works: A Look at the Legislative Branch*. Minneapolis: Lerner Publications, 2004.

Fish, Bruce, and Becky Druost Fish. *The Speaker of the House of Representatives*. Your Government and How It Works series. New York: Chelsea House, 2001.

Koestler-Grack, Rachel. *The House of Representatives*. The U.S. Government: How It Works series. New York: Chelsea House, 2007.

Speaker Nancy Pelosi
http://www.speaker.gov
Nancy Pelosi's website contains information about the office of Speaker, as well as Pelosi herself. Click on the Kid's Page for some interesting activities.

ACKNOWLEDGMENTS

Acknowledgements: Many thanks go to Drew Hammill in the Speaker's office; Alexandra and Christine Pelosi; Scott Gerber in Senator Feinstein's office; Linnea Michel; editor extraordinaire Jean Reynolds; Steve, Zoe, and Abby McElroy; the faculties and staffs of Southern New England School of Law and Drexel University College of Law.

INDEX

Page numbers in *italics* refer to illustrations.